I0436900

Welcome to My World

by

Patrice

authorHOUSE®

AuthorHouse™
1663 Liberty Drive, Suite 200
Bloomington, IN 47403
www.authorhouse.com
Phone: 1-800-839-8640

© 2008 Patrice. All rights reserved.

No part of this book may be reproduced, stored in a retrieval system, or transmitted by any means without the written permission of the author.

First published by AuthorHouse 9/9/2008

ISBN: 978-1-4343-0982-2 (sc)

Library of Congress Control Number: 2007909489

Printed in the United States of America
Bloomington, Indiana

This book is printed on acid-free paper.

Dedication

To my family and friends and
all the people who have touched my life.
Without you this book would not exist.

Table of Contents

Foreword

Poetry is unique
in that it's true meaning is
known only to its author.

Language may allow the reader to formulate an understanding
and to determine a broad meaning but the pain, happiness and
emotion that sparked and gave life to each poem lives only in
the mind of the writer...

The intent of each piece is to share an emotional or physical
event, to recall a feeling the reader may have experienced or
to ignite a feeling for the reader to briefly walk in the writer's
shoes. Shining new light onto the experience.

Overtones

I have spent much of my life writing poetry for my self - expression without the vulnerability of identity. After all how could I be vulnerable and show weakness. I am the "band-aid" child in my family keeping everyone together, I am the best friend who can always be counted on to be there in a time of need. The problems and needs of everyone else always come before mine with one exception, I need to be able to look back on my life and not be staring at a pile of regrets. This overriding goal has driven me to experience my feelings passionately; anger, love, sensuality, sadness the full spectrum of emotions. I believe we must all feel first so that we can make logical and rational decisions without regrets.

I learned early on that sex equaled power on a variety of levels, most importantly power over your own body. Something people lose sight of is the power over our own bodies, the power to shape it, work it, live in it and the power of reproduction and sexuality. My body is the one thing on this planet that I truly own. For years I approached sex and sexuality with a totally disconnected attitude. Unfortunately, when you're not emotionally involved in your actions, good, bad or indifferent, you're not able to make sound judgments and decisions which makes each disconnected situation an ideal place for regrets.

Throughout much of my life my relationships have had negative overtones. I have been bitter, and couldn't see that I was part of the reason that these things were happening to me. I had lost or more specifically surrendered my control over my own body and handed over that control with less scrutiny than I would give selecting an outfit to go out on a Saturday night. Now as I face hitting middle age I have finally reached a point where I maintain control of my body and I can except who I am.

I am a woman who doesn't fit neatly into any stereotype
❖ I am the unconventional mom in almost every school crowd
❖ I am a career woman whose mind must be stimulated to be happy
❖ I am the best friend I always wanted
❖ I am pushy, bossy, demanding, and loud
❖ I am me.
Strengths and flaws in all
❖ To be molded by me
❖ To make my own decisions
❖ To not accept societal restrictions
❖ To do what makes me happy
To be simply, Patrice.

This book is my poetic expression of my life over the last 20 years. The loves I've found, surrendered control to and the heartaches that helped me reach down once more and pick up that control.

Life

Life

folded faces by and by

empty spaces come up dry

people moving through the streets

time and love at once are beat

a clear sea is far from view

darkness and silence shining through

opening doors are what we see

shattered images of you and me

we live by wants die by needs

blood and lust all for the lead

sleeping cries escape our ears

bold faces showing only fear

Love Songs

See through the darkness
What will we find
A tattered image
A worn out mind

An ongoing maze
Another dead end
Is there an answer
Around the bend

See the eyes
Crying in the night
A hopeless journey
No time to fight

Struggle with emotions
Are there any reasons
Nothing stays the same
Like the change of the seasons

Where are you now
Dreaming of the day
All my times just waiting
When love will come my way

Helpless

Try for a time
When I can be
The one I want
A time for me

An endless journey
Fighting lines
Can't break through
I've made my mind

Against the Odds

It's a wonder
          how we make it
Through this life
          we lead on strings
Falling forever falling
          try to make it
Straight for the top
          one more step

Before you hit bottom

Trip

Faster than the speed limit
Never-ending flow
Can't escape the tears you've cried
Nothing left of serenity
Blowing thoughtless dreams
We become the lost light
Searching for others of our kind.

Dreams

Misdealt the dreams
of our fortune
Destiny miles
from our reach
Striving for
ecstasy
Wanting more
and more
Painfully struck
pleasure
Screams within
our hearts.

Twisted Fate

Endless hope forgotten love
Never remember what we see
Seeking resistance high above
Lost feelings drown in the midst

Glaring down among the stars
Unraveling wraths appear
Spirits gathering from afar
Tripping seeds of thought

Watched and withered by the sight
Always forever falling
We the children lose our might
Weakened we fall to our knees

Blood flowing from our minds
The experience lost in time
Eternity ends, started a new kind
Life has come to an end.

Things on My Mind

Vengeance
Strives within
Bubbling over
Seeping out
Maybe...not today
Maybe tomorrow
Could be next year
Could be ten
Sooner or later
It all comes out
Striking back
For all those times
When I was down
And you kept
Walking over.

Frustration

Working my way through the day
Just can't seem to get no where.

Try my best to make the effort
Nobody listens I keep telling what it's all about

Can't seem to get my way.
No more reason just bitching and complaining.

The days been wasted no way out
Try for a time when I can be the one

An endless journey fighting lines
Can't break through I've made my mind.

Life Goes On

As the day goes wandering
Wondering what to do
Can you see these images
Tell you what to do

My eyes see the danger
The sorrow and the pain
I can't help but want to
Think we're all insane

Do you know the answer
Deep inside your head
It's there for you to remember
Exactly what I said

Reality, Reality

My heart screams
calling your name.

My eyes search
trying to find you.

My hands fumble
desperately in the dark

I reach for you
but you're not there

Reality mocks me.

Decision

Ripping and tearing
at what I know is right

Fighting choices
I always swore against.

Yet desire and wanting
reach for satiation.

Regrets

A day of sorrow
for fears and dreams
something missing
do you know what I mean

        Screaming thoughts
        of secret wishes
        no one hears
        or even listens

Don't know why
I have these feelings
wasting time
my heart's been stealing

        Shallow images
        a forgotten story
        another day past
        we live for glory

Faith

Its time,

time again,

to try your

will...

a faith

you have,

tried and

true.

Make

your way,

to

someone

new.

Friend ?

People except me
        the way I've been,
so except me now
        as I
commit another sin.

Life Stars

Sometimes a star shines on us

Bringing people into our lives

That we will hold forever in our hearts.

Chivalry

A sweet song of love
fills the air we breathe
A knight in shining armor
defends his maidens honor
Sparks fly and fire glows
shadows of a battle gone by
For love and glory we fight
and die.

Autumn Flight

I dreamed a dream
      of thoughtless things
      of being little once again
      of wild imaginations
      of never ending dreams
      of mischievous times
      of being little once again
      of big balloons
I dreamed a dream

Times have changed
      and so have I
      no more dreams
      or mischievous times
      or big balloons
      or autumn leaves
      its just me and
      my imagination
      running free

Then & Now

An everyday meeting
changes an ordinary day
into one to celebrate

A meeting that
grew through friendship
to a bond for life

A person that I
cannot ever imagine
living my life without

Though breadth and depth
may change over time
the connection will last

Forever

Never Forget

Some things are beyond words
True friends stand the test of time
Through smiles and tears
Support and celebration

Sharing trust and respect
Unconditional understanding
Whether we talk, visit or
Just hold memories close

One thing for certain is
Our connection for life

6-24-05

May the sunshine
        In your life
Overshadow the rain

May the warmth
        On your face
Keep the cold at bay

May the happiness
        You feel
Outweigh any sorrow

May each day
        That we celebrate
Fulfill your desires.

Birthday

Look back on your
life with pride

Look forward to the future
with excitement

Don't hesitate,
act on your ideas

Experience each day
without regret

And love with all
that you have.

Dreaming

Dreaming,
does the dream always
have to end...
Why not last forever.
A sweet dream,
to escape a world
filled with anger and fear.
An exotic place
made for lovers,
where love can last forever.
If only it were possible,
to live a dream...
A perfect time,
a perfect place.
Where the end of one dream,
is the beginning of the next.

Spirits

Spirits in the night,

can you feel them

in the air...

Maybe it's someone

you used to know,

maybe I know too.

Pass through

your body

leave you cold and scared.

Waiting for the morning

can you see them there...

pushing round

that wheel of time,

coming back for more.

Spirits in the night,

can you feel them in the air...

Confusion

Tides of emotion
ebb and flow
seeping into
all that I am.

Decisions
waiver with
rejection and
compassion

Competing for
acceptance,
An absolution
of future journeys.

Rise of the New Patriots

A subconscious haze
Filters and processes the pain
So close, yet so far away
Shards of reality seep through

Eyes blinded by hate
Tear washed faces
Grieving for the needless deaths
Foreboding, uncertainty

A shared embrace weeps
For all the families
Torn by violence
Never to embrace again.

Unspeakable acts
Spoken out loud
As if to give them life
Offended and enraged

The ultimate betrayal
Senseless death and destruction
In spite of it all
Spirits defy the injustice

All enveloping pride
Unites patriots of old with the new
An emerging sense of belonging
Protection for all

Brothers born of pride
One race, human
One people, American
One Nation, America
Under God.

9/12/2001

Mortality

Hate

Spirit

Pride

Defiance

Anxiety

My brain aches
      My mind is spinning
      I can't find my way
      Through clear skies
      Darkness brings on desperation
      Clouding all judgement

I want to feel
      To have a sense of control
      To live again like myself

I want to be me again.

Anxiety Overruled

Each day
I put on
My face
      Swallow down
      The ball in
      My throat
            And carry
            Forward
            My smile

Reflections

My eyes show your feelings
a reflection of your face
A place you can't escape
the person who you are
Every time you look away
or even close your eyes
You are sure to find yourself
the next time you meet mine

I will still be there
looking back at you
For your eyes hold my mirror
I see myself in you
Are they true reflections
of who we are together
Somehow we are connected
afraid of what it means.

Love

Love Happens

Sometimes when you least expect it
Love grabs you by the collar and
Throws you to the ground.

It kicks you in the face,
Twists a knife in your heart,
Screaming to be acknowledged.

It leaves you bloody and beaten.
Still you try to pick yourself up
Struggling to break free

But no matter how hard you fight
Love will always overpower
Stripping you of defenses

Forcing you to surrender.

Creeping In

Each day brought
A new intensity
An obsession thinking
About you constantly

Without warning
I lost my heart
I didn't notice it was gone
Until I saw you pick it up

I was surprised
By what happened
Shocked I didn't see it coming,
That I wasn't even looking

Swept Away

When I look around
At where I am
Sweet, kind people
Surround me
Loving me their way

I have given
My love and friendship
Freely
But my heart
Was swept away

Surprise

We talked over the years
Our time together grew
We spent hours talking
About everything and nothing

From an occasional meeting
To a daily routine
One day I left you and
Couldn't think of anything else

You drifted through my
Mind somehow relating
To everything
Encountered.

You smiled and said
Kind words
Locking eyes
A bit longer than usual

Conversations continued on
But the atmosphere seemed
To change.

Why Me

It's the way you pay
attention to everything
about me

It's the way you
laugh with me and share
your deepest emotions

It's the way we have
so much in common and
admire our differences

It's the way you know
what I want, think and feel
without my saying

It's the way you accept me
flaws and all with an
unmistakable sincerity

It's the way you help me
to look inside and
find strength in myself

It's the way I know
you're always there for me
whatever I need

It's the way you look at me
with an emotional intensity
kind and caring

It's the way you touch me
with tenderness, deliberate
and intentional

It's the way everything
about you turns me on
unleashing all inhibitions

It's the way we are
together.... whole,
made for each other

One Way or Another

I open my heart
and soul to you
I share them freely
with new found generosity

Your are the truest
of friends
My heart finds comfort
in your hands

Even when we
are at odds
I need you
to comfort me

I have found
a passion and warmth
unmatched in my life

A love, a friend
worth more than
words can say

Forever yours.

White Shoulders

Soft features reminisce
A halo of past memories
Blurred and haunting
Through the diamond glass

Drawn against my will
Trembling, resistance flees
A chance gaze pierces
Thick smokey curtains.

Music, voices and sound
Blend and fade behind
Oblivion encompasses all
Existence is you and me

Things I long forgot
Reach up from my soul
Seeping into the moment
Frightened I retreat

Defiance leads me away
Conversation is shallow
Time stands still
Blackness swallows the room

Blinded by a white shoulder
Grazing past mine
Searching for intention
Lost in desperation

Thunderous pounding hearts
Desperate to avoid synchrony
Pass swearing alliance
Through a sea of empty promises

I Am Yours

Love me hard
Make you yours
Hold me tight
Don't let go
Carry me through
Till we are one.

I Need You

Deep breaths
Help to control
The rise and fall
Of emotions

Everywhere I look
Everything I see
Reminds me of you

Try as I might
I can't chase
You from my thoughts

I feel an
Overwhelming
Sense of rightness
Belonging.

You & I

A simple heartbeat
a calming sense of being
a powerful force of life

Beating slowing beating
without logic or thought
the steady strong pace
a feeling of love so strong
tears well up in my eyes
holding, squeezing
afraid to let go
least you get away.

A connection,
beyond words.
A knowing,
across lifetimes.

Heartfelt

Desperation
Anxiety
A broken heart

Longing
Anticipation
A lonely heart

Respect
Desire
A heart in love

Bittersweet

Each time I think of you
my eyes well as a smile
stretches across my face

Sensations are bittersweet
gentle warming rushes through
while longing tugs at my heart

Today

Holding tightly,
to what might be

Wanting to see you,
...dancing with patience

I choke back tears,
hoping to hear your voice

Desperately seeking,
affirmation of us

Anxiety overshadows,
everything before me

Longing for a reality,
to match my desire.

Heartache

Afar

Sadness finds its way
to my heart again

Try as I might nothing
waivers its strength

The empty feeling in
my soul aches for you

Each day that passes
can never be regained

Embrace the moment
and your happiness

Because they both
may slip away.

Sins in the Night

My heart bleeds
an open wound,
tears overcome
my struggle with
what I know is right.
I created my hell
and suffer my pains,
the agony is excruciating.
My body aches,
my mind is reeling,
the pain is punishment
for what I've done or
afraid to do.
It is merciless and brutal,
paralyzing my life.

Secret Lover

As I walk away,

tears well in my eyes.

The emptiness in my chest

is overwhelming.

> My heart aches with desperation
>
> and the fear of
>
> not knowing whether
>
> you'll ever love me back,
>
> or if you even know,
>
> I love you.

You are my soul mate

but life's choices keep us apart.

Admiring from afar,

teasing reality with chance encounters.

Satisfy immediate needs,

cutting deeper, multiplying the pain.

Crush

Without disruption
the pain will
continue to grow

Some days are unbearable
I weep for all that
my heart desires

Secret

My heart aches daily
  as we part
Our choices seem
  a cruel mockery
A barrier keeping
  us apart
So many lives
  caught in the balance
So many lives
  to be disrupted
Death of our lives
  to begin anew

Lost

Crying eyes
        sadness unfolds
Gripping my heart
        choking me.

Shortness of life
        sacrifices untold
Desperate for realization
        haunting memories.

To live and die
        An eternal fight
With all reality

Breaking through
        The walls
Searching for tomorrow

Deceit

Cry Cry.
        Feel it build up inside
Feel the hurt as it tears
        you inside.
Make love to me
        as you see
someone else inside.

Close your eyes
        when you touch me
So you can pretend
        that she is here.

Guilt

Love is blind
Fear overrules
Striking back
At those we love
To protect ourselves
From the unknown

Broken Heart

Misty eyed
I stare out the window

Can't believe its time to go

Broken promises
And broken dreams

Desperate to forget
Mistakes that were made

Can't change the past

Where do you go
From a place with no doors

Searching for the
Strength to carry on

Blindness leads the way

Time will mend the wounds
With tears and loneliness.

Love Loss

From deep inside you
It screams to get out

Ripping-tearing at the heart
Sending wild messages
Disrupting the brain
Seizing common sense
Releases rabid thought

Whole emptiness engulfs the soul
Suffer great defeats
refuse to die
Repeated deaths strike again
Crushing the structure of essence

Shreading shreads of empty soul
Full to the bodies' walls with rage.

Another Day

Another day
Another time gone by

One more moment
Before I die

Can't see tomorrow
Blinded by today

Looking for an answer
That's no where in sight

Can't you see
What's inside of me

All the pain
All the sorrow

People always answer
But there's no one there

Try to hide
In empty space

Watch me disappear.

Change

The shining light of the moonlit sky
Wondering always why

Try to answer but no one hears
So many questions fall on deaf ears

The distance between us seems to grow.
I'll never know why you hide your feelings

To make a point or simply cry
Again I wonder why?

Spent

Show me now
What I don't know
Make me see
What I can't
Let me feel
I'm so cold
Tell me why
I can't cry

I Give Up

World, world
See me cry

Watch my eyes
They won't dry

Feel my body
Strong no more

Helplessness
Has barred the door

Now this time
My life is fading

Can't you see
No more waiting.

Rumors

Gonna make you listen
See it my way
It's over now
Don't waste another day

        Jealousy the reason
        Why we don't win
        Blinded visions
        Living to sin

Dirty little secrets
Never meant to hear
Shadowed eyes
Telling every ear

        You're guilty of lies
        I'm running scared
        Can't stop tryin
        To make you aware

You always seem to worry
Emotions filled with fear
I always say I'm sorry
For what I have no idea

        I'll make the decision
        The time is right
        To stop your complainin
        And end this fight.

Bad Choices

Try to find the answers
All my loves in vain
Why all the hurting
Why all the pain

I'd give the world for you
Just to see you smile
To have you by my side
Even for a short while

Alone again, without you
Never know if you'll be back
Praying for us to be happy
Hoping you won't pack

All I want is you
Can't bear to be alone
Don't know if I can make it
My hearts cut to the bone.

Affair

Dream another day
Blank expressions
Minds torn in two
Can't find a way

Fight for a time
No explanation
I wonder why
Lessons all mine

No more feeling
Blinded eyes
Lost in love
Hearts not healing

Live and learn

Betrayal

All the questions
All those lines
To make me feel
Torn up inside

All the anger
All the pain
There's no end
Just beginning again

Can't you hear
Hear what I'm saying
I'm through with you
And the game you're playin

There are no answers
It's all the same
An endless battle
You'll never change

My Twisted Mind

A sleeping dream
A crying tear
All that we have
To fear

A love that's lost
A shattered hope
Forgotten times
Of happy cheers

Remembering
What's near
Broken pieces
A lonely soul

The scavengers
Pick you apart
Destroy anything
Whole

As the pieces
Become dust
Swept together
In circles they go

Twisted and distorted
It takes shape
A piece of mind.

Love ?

You hate me with love
You hit me with tears
       I cry for you
       I'd die for you
You tear me up
You lift me down
       I shake with fear
       I love you still

A Question of Love

Is there warning
or does it just fade away

Those times we shared
soon to be forgot

Why does something of joy
cause the greatest sorrow

Is it possible that our feelings
change overnight

The tears we shared
soon to separate

Can we stop this
viscous cycle of broken hearts

Is there an end
to all this pain?

There is only hope that the time
Between start and finish will be forever.

Missing You

My heart aches
       For my love
Calling out your name
       Searching for your face
You touch my soul
       In ways,
I never dreamed possible.

Time to Go

Today we move forward
looking back on yesterday
unable to let go

Emotional chains tie us down
hold us back from the future
at the tips of our fingers

Intimacy

Heart Strings

Sometimes two faces
meet in the dark
Afraid of what they
find there
A spark ignites
and our bodies
become one...

You pull on my
heart strings
Every time
I hear your voice
or feel you
by my side.

Passion dances
behind my eyes,
teasing reality
with little white
lies.

Desire Exposed

Your eyes see through me
with compassion and desire;
cradling my being
outstretched on high
pulling back each layer
of facade.

Admiring the bareness
of all that is exposed.
Shaking and scared,
I willingly stare back.
My chest heaves with
anticipation and
fear of rejection.

My heart races
trying to keep pace,
torn between the past
and the future.
Passion ignites
from every touch, stare
and smile.

Holding on
to possibilities,
never to let go.

Awakening

Skin to skin
senses burning
each touch
electrifying,
taking over..

Heat rising
to the surface
stretching
over my body,
lingering..

A light caress
daring to
explore
unknown pleasures,
longing for more..

Breathless

Partners

Every once in a while
>   I yearn for you.
I can feel your warm body
>   wrapped around mine.
To smother me with
>   your heat.
The sweet taste
>   of your sweat.
The feeling deep inside,
>   of union.
Every once in a while
>   I yearn for you.
To pass away the summer nights,
>   ...or any night.

Only You

A glimpse of you,
        out of the corner of my eye
        sends blood rushing
        through my veins

Flush cheeks,
crest my line of sight

Our eyes speak,
sharing each rush of emotion

Words and surroundings,
fade into one another

Every move you make,
takes my breath away

Each time you touch me,
the sensation ripples over my skin

        The feel of you in my hand
        resonates between my legs
        deep into my body,
always wanting more.

Yearning

I lay naked and exposed
hungry and wanting
I watch you undress and
lay your body next to mine

I flush as you draw your
finger the length of my face
My heart quickens as you
kiss your way to my breasts

Anticipation grows as I
feel your breath on my neck and
The warmth of your skin
stretching from head to toe

You slowly part my legs and
nestle your body between them
I am hot and breathless
my desire runs over

Waves of sensations overpower

Lullaby

In a sea of gray
our bodies
twist, wrap, meld
together.
Each becoming part
of the other,
beginning and end
indistinguishable.
Hearts beat in unison
sound like thunder.
Passion raging, burning,
tension mounting,
seething, urging,
struggling to get
free.

Rainbows
and waves of color
wash down
wrapping content
and satisfaction
around.
Deep sighs overcome
the thunderous heart.
Soft breath
fills your chest,
the nights lullaby.

Unspoken

The way you look at me
with eyes so innocent

The way you touch me
every inch of my body comes alive

The way passion burns
through every kiss

The way you feel
when we become one

The way ecstasy
erupts from each union

The way you satisfy, and leave
me wanting at each parting

The way you always know
what I'm going to say

The way a smile says
I love you....

Remember

From the minute
        my eyes lose your sight
I miss you
        with an intensity beyond words
My heart aches
        longing for you

Desires, passions and emotions
        shared without speaking
The intoxicating way
        you smell, feel and taste
A wanton smile
        drawing me in

The pure sensuality
        of a simple caress.

Epilogue

This collection starts with the darkness and smallness of "Life". My fifteen year old self's confrontation with:

- The pain that comes with loving another
- The insignificance of one person's life within and across humanity over time.
- The cruelty that lives in people
- The desperation of wanting and not knowing one's purpose.

I will close the collection with "Life" once again but from the perspective of a near forty-year old woman's understanding of:

- That pain that tells us we experienced the most beautiful emotional and physical event a human can experience.
- The significance one person can make in influencing those around them and how the effect can be multiplied forward with each new sharing.
- The overwhelming kindness that lives in ALL people.
- My purpose in life and in each relationship.

Sometimes you have to look a little deeper and try a little harder to find what you're looking for. In the end the only thing that matters is that you allow yourself to feel, to follow your heart even when it doesn't make sense – to be true to yourself.

Life

folded faces by and by

empty spaces come up dry

people moving through the streets

time and love at once are beat

a clear sea is far from view

darkness and silence shining through

opening doors are what we see

shattered images of you and me

we live by wants die by needs

blood and lust all for the lead

sleeping cries escape our ears

bold faces showing only fear

www.ingramcontent.com/pod-product-compliance
Lightning Source LLC
Chambersburg PA
CBHW031250280526
45784CB00004B/1793